CW01086420

A Brief History of

WARGRAVE

Edited by

Peter Halman and Peter Delaney

Wargrave Local History Society

© 2019 Wargrave Local History Society

Published by Wargrave Local History Society, Wargrave, Berkshire

www.wargravehistory.org.uk

All rights reserved. No part of this publication may be reproduced, stored in a retrieval system or transmitted in any form or by any means, electronic, mechanical, photocopying, recording or otherwise, without the prior permission of the Wargrave Local History Society.

ISBN   978 0 9511878 6 9

Editorial notes

The contents of this publication draw heavily upon the work of the authors of *The Book of Wargrave* and *The Second Book of Wargrave* and the editors gratefully acknowledge their contribution.

A number of the images used are from our collection of postcards, many of which are more than a hundred years old. Inevitably, some have been damaged or marked and we have made careful and sympathetic use of computer software to restore them to a little nearer their original condition. No material changes have been made and we would be happy to open our archives to any reader who wishes to inspect the original prints.

The drawing of the Woodclyffe Hall is reproduced by kind permission of Sally Castle (www.sallycastle.co.uk).

Contents

Village history

The earliest authentic reference to Wargrave appears in the Domesday Book of 1086, the great survey ordered by William the Conqueror to record the details of his newly-acquired kingdom. This tells us that the village was already well established at that time and the manor of around 500 acres had a population of approximately 1,000 people. There was also a mill and three 'fisheries', with eel traps or weirs. The total value of the manor was recorded as being £27, making it one of the most valuable in this part of Berkshire. The land now belonged to the new king but had previously been the property of Queen Edith, the wife of King Edward the Confessor.

Why 'Wargrave'?
Visitors often ask to which war does the name refer and whose is the grave. The answer is nothing to do with either. The village stood on the edge of Windsor Forest with plentiful groves of trees and its three weirs, giving us Weirgrove and several other variations on that theme.

The heart of the village
Although we do not have firm archaeological evidence, it is reasonable to assume that the centre of the early village was the church and Mill Green, near to the river. The site of the mill mentioned in the Domesday Book has still to be confirmed, but it is likely to have been around the area where the River Loddon joins the Thames. Undulations on Mill Green suggest the earlier presence of a simple street, but this also has still to be established. Parts of nearby Wargrave Court date from the fifteenth century and the building could well have been the centre of local administration and justice for the Lord of the Manor.

One other building which might also have been the manor house was popularly known as Queen Emma's Palace. This stood in Church Street until 1827. Queen Emma is said to have lived in Wargrave, but if so, this wasn't her palace. She was a Saxon queen and this engraving is of a Tudor house, built 400 years after her time. The site is now occupied by the Woodclyffe Hostel.

The later medieval village

During the thirteenth century, the layout of the village began to take the shape we recognise today. Houses along the High Street were established as 'Burgage Plots', with long narrow gardens and rear access via Ferry Lane or Backsideans. The oldest house is believed to be Timber Cottage, opposite the Woodclyffe Hall. Over the years, the High Street has developed in a variety of styles but still retains its medieval property boundaries.

Ownership of the Manor lands

The manor of Wargrave was owned by successive Bishops of Winchester. In 1529, Cardinal Wolsey, then also Bishop of Winchester, fell out with Henry VIII and the manor passed to the Crown. In 1558, Queen Elizabeth granted the manor to the Neville family, whose descendants, the Lords Braybrooke, remained Lords of the Manor until 1891 and were significant benefactors to the village. The house which is now known as Wargrave Manor was originally called Wargrave Hill and was built in the 1780s. It has never been the manor in the feudal sense.

A rural community

In many ways, everyday life in the village changed surprisingly little from medieval times until the Victorian era, when the effects of the agricultural and industrial revolutions were felt. The nineteenth century also brought important changes with the building of new and larger schools, the arrival of the railway, the development of leisure activities associated with the river and, in the early twentieth century, the profound social consequences of the First World War.

Sheep dipping at the St George and Dragon ferry

3

A tale of two rivers

From the earliest times until late in the nineteenth century, the River Thames played an important and, in some cases, dominant role in the life of the community. As well as being an important source of food through its eel traps, the river was the main highway for trade and travel before the coming of the railway and the construction of better roads. Many everyday necessities such as coal, timber and stone were delivered by barges to the village wharves. The barges were sailed, or hauled by draught horses or gangs of men.

Better control of the river was achieved in the early 1800s when more modern locks were built, reducing the flooding of lower-lying outskirts of the village. Our busiest wharf adjoined the St George and Dragon, where the Wyatt family had set up in business in the 1840s, running a hotel, wharf, ferry and boatyard.

The social scene

The coming of the railway soon brought commercial river traffic to an end, but the train service enabled people to travel much more easily and quickly from London to riverside towns such as Maidenhead, Marlow and Henley. The Edwardian era was the heyday of the river's popularity, which led to the growth of these newly fashionable destinations.

Many lovely houses were built along the river banks and Wargrave was also home to a number of houseboats, some of them very grand. A favourite spot was on its second river, the Loddon, which rises in the Basingstoke area and joins the Thames near to Wargrave railway station.

Wargrave and Shiplake Regatta

This annual event was established in 1867 and has always maintained its popularity. It is a traditional boat regatta and is the second largest on the Thames, attracting many entrants in a variety of categories. The focus is more on local and family boating than on the international aspect of Henley Royal Regatta. Despite this, as you can see, our local regatta used to be a much more formal affair than today's relaxed style. One of the regatta features is a ferry running between the St George and Dragon and the Shiplake water meadows. There was once a regular daily ferry across to Shiplake which started in 1837. Before then, a waterman offered a service running from the end of Ferry Lane, off Church Street.

Local boating

The Wargrave Boating Club dates from 1949 when it specialised in boating with punts, skiffs and Canadian canoes. The club took a major step forward in the 1970s when a new clubhouse was built adjoining the boathouse, attracting many new members. Special emphasis has always been placed on encouraging children to learn boating skills in a safe environment through training and participation in competitive events. Parents join their children in many of the club's activities.

An attractive quiet corner for boating can still be found along Hennerton Backwater, formed by the Thames dividing just below the St George and Dragon and running for about a mile before rejoining the main stream above Marsh Lock, on the way to Henley. Only the smallest craft can negotiate the backwater, resulting in a relatively uncrowded and peaceful experience for those using oars or paddles.

Notable buildings

St Mary's Church

Certainly the oldest and most important building in the village, the parish church has been a focal point of the community for close to a thousand years. The north wall and doorway of the church date from the twelfth century and the elegant brick-clad tower was built in 1635, but most of the structure was rebuilt and some parts enlarged after the disastrous fire in 1914. The interior and the churchyard have memorials of differing styles which remind us of noteworthy villagers. Among them is an unusual stone tomb, supported on metal feet. This is dedicated to James Leigh-Perrot and his wife Jane, who was Jane Austen's aunt. Nearby is the badly-worn gravestone of Elizabeth Tussaud, wife of the famous Madame Tussaud's grandson.

Near to the wall on the west side of the churchyard are several tombs of the Ximenes family. Sir Maurice Ximenes founded the Wargrave Rangers in 1801, a local militia which became part of the Berkshire Yeomanry Cavalry just before the Battle of Waterloo. Against the church wall, near to the lych gate, there are several tombs of the Piggott family who were important benefactors and gave us our first school. Also near to the lych gate is an unusual brick-built vault, the Hannen Columbarium, looking rather like a dovecote. This was designed by the eminent architect, Sir Edwin Lutyens, for the Hannen family, who lived in the village. Our elegant war memorial cross on Mill Green was built to Sir Edwin's design.

The church fire in 1914

Although not proven, there was strong circumstantial evidence that fires had been started in several places by militant suffragettes. Despite being damaged, the tower survived, but it acted as a chimney which led to the

clock mechanism and the bells falling to the floor. The original bell clappers, distorted by the heat of the fire, can be seen hanging on the wall inside the base of the tower as a dramatic reminder. Fortunately, the church registers, lectern and silver plate were saved.

Wargrave Court

This lovely old house stands near to the church on Mill Green. The earliest parts of the building date from the fifteenth century and it was

extended and altered in later years. It is thought most likely that it was effectively the village's original manor house, due to its proximity to the river, the church and the possible site of the mill. More recently, many villagers have enjoyed the beautiful gardens where concerts and other events have been staged.

The Bull and the Greyhound

These two old pubs have faced each other at the crossroads in the the High Street for a very long time. The Bull is said to date from the fifteenth century and its large old oak beams are impressive. To add to the atmosphere, it is also reputed to have a resident ghost.

The Greyhound is younger than its rival across the road, having been built in the early eighteenth century. The Manor Court met here from time to time, instead of at Waltham St Lawrence. One of the village dairies was at the side of the Greyhound on the High Street and the village blacksmith was next door on School Lane. The smithy workshop has been preserved.

The Woodclyffe Hostel

Now the home of the library, the snooker club and the Sansom Room, the Hostel in Church Street was originally built in 1905 as a Working Men's Club to act as a counter-attraction to the seven pubs which were in the High Street at one time. During the First World War, it served as

a recovery hospital for twenty convalescing soldiers. The nursing staff was provided by members of the Wargrave Voluntary Aid Detachment and a plaque on the front of the building reminds us of those local ladies. The Hostel also had a bathroom available for the use of those villagers who did not have one at home.

The Woodclyffe Hall

There is a wide range of architectural styles in the High Street but the Woodclyffe Hall stands out, with its distinctive Arts & Crafts design by Cole Adams. It was built in 1900 on the site of an old malt house and was the gift of Mrs Harriette Cooke Smith, one of the village's most important benefactors. It is a Grade II Listed Building, indicating its architectural merit. Over the years it has served as the Village Hall, a theatre, a polling station, a military hospital during the 1914-18 war and the venue for countless other meetings and functions, both public and private. It underwent extensive refurbishment and renovation during 2017-18 and is now the home of Wargrave's much-admired Theatre Workshop.

The St George and Dragon

It's likely that the majority of people who pass through Wargrave will notice the St George and Dragon hostelry with its splendid riverside location: almost the only place in the village with publicly accessible river frontage. Three generations of the very well-known Wyatt family ran the hotel, a boat business and a commercial wharf which imported coal

and a range of general merchandise. They also ran the ferry to Shiplake which had been moved from Ferry Lane, off Church Street, in 1837. Eventually, the hotel/pub was sold to the brewers and the Wyatts concentrated on their boatyard business.

In one sense, the St George and Dragon was world famous. Lovers of nineteenth-century light reading would have enjoyed the comments about Wargrave and its riverside hotel in the comic novel, *Three Men in a Boat*, by Jerome K Jerome. The book was first published in 1889 and became an immediate bestseller, particularly in Britain and the United States. It has never been out of print.

Wargrave Manor

This is undoubtedly the grandest house in the village and stands in an unrivalled position. It was built in the 1780s by Joseph Hill, a London lawyer and member of the prominent Jekyll family, who named it Wargrave Hill. In the 1860s it was home to Gertrude Jekyll, an artist who became one of the leading garden designers of the Victorian era. She also worked closely with Sir Edwin Lutyens. Several different families owned or rented the house in later years,

including Sir William Cain who renamed it Wargrave Manor in 1918. The Manor can only be seen by looking up the hill from the main road just beyond the St George and Dragon. For the past 40 years it has been the property of His Majesty the Sultan of Oman.

Timber Cottage

Although it doesn't look like it, 67 High Street is probably the oldest house in the village and stands almost opposite the Woodclyffe Hall. Hidden behind the early twentieth century gable is a fine mid-fourteenth

century timber-framed building. It was originally a hall house, with an earth floor, a fire in the centre and no chimney; the smoke finding its way out through the rafters. The floor over the hall would have been added later to increase the accommodation. We tend to think of half-timbered houses as being of Tudor design, but this building was already more than a hundred years old when the Tudor kings arrived.

Over more recent years, the cottage has served as a butcher's, a bicycle shop and a tea parlour.

The railway

Brunel's Great Western railway line between London and Bristol was opened in 1841 and the branch line from Twyford to Henley was opened in 1857. The coming of the railway had put an end to Henley's thriving commercial river and stagecoach traffic, but the regatta was established in 1839 and in 1851 Prince Albert became its patron, giving the event a coveted 'royal' prefix. The event became highly fashionable and the railway made it easy to travel from London.

Although villagers could see trains crossing the river on the wooden viaduct, there was no station at Wargrave until 1900, despite repeated requests to the GWR. Station Road was built to give access from the High Street. Prior to that, the nearest station was at Shiplake, via a ferry from Willow Lane.

The photograph below was taken quite soon after Wargrave station opened and shows two platforms, a footbridge and substantial station buildings. Goods traffic included newspapers for W H Smith, fresh fish packed in ice and also coal, formerly brought by barges. In later years, the siding was used during the summer for camping coaches.

As with so many branch lines, there was a long-term reduction in facilities following various rail reorganisation programmes and the last original building was demolished in 1985.

The Piggott schools

Although there was some schooling in Wargrave in the seventeenth century, Robert Piggott's will, drawn up in 1796, laid the foundation for wider and more structured education of village children. He left a large sum of money in trust to establish two schools, one for 20 boys and the other for 20 girls of the Parish of Wargrave, whose parents could not afford to pay for their education. The first schools occupied two cottages in the High Street, which are still standing. In 1828 they moved to the lower part of Victoria Road, sharing the premises of the National School.

To meet the increasing demand for places, a new school, combining the two original ones, was built on School Hill in 1862, eventually becoming today's Junior School. Separate provision for infants was established in 1910 in the former District School buildings in Victoria Road on the site now occupied by Elizabeth Court and the Medical Centre. This school was moved to brand-new premises in Beverley Gardens in 1963. Also in the 1960s, Crazies Hill School was replaced by a new and larger building.

During the period between the two World Wars, increasing population and raising of the school leaving age created the need for more places for older pupils. Government legislation also required local authorities to make greater provision. As a result, the Piggott Senior School was opened in 1940. Its aim was to provide senior education for children from Wargrave and surrounding communities. The school's founders would have been surprised to see the range of its modern facilities and to learn that the school now has 1500 students.

The story of schooling in Wargrave is in many respects like that of other similar towns and villages. The early foundation was largely administered by the Vicar and Churchwardens. They supervised the school and with the Trustees chose the Piggott scholars. The gifts of notable citizens are recorded but many others gave generously in their own way and have contributed to the education of our children.

11

Historical buildings and places

1. St Mary's Church

2. Wargrave Court

3. The Village Pound - an enclosure for stray animals.

4. The North Star Inn is now Star Cottage.

5. The White Horse Inn is now Tudor Cottage.

6. The Bull Hotel, probably dating from the fifteenth century.

7. The Woodclyffe Hostel is now home to the library and snooker club.

8. The Greyhound and the former village blacksmiths's forge.

9. The Woodclyffe Hall

10. Timber Cottage, probably the oldest house in the village.

11. The White Hart hotel and pub is now a restaurant.

12. The non-conformist chapel is now a private house.

13. The Red Lion Beer House is now Jessamine Cottage.

14. Wargrave Hall was associated with senior politicians 100 years ago.

15. The Woodclyffe Almshouses were once part of a military academy.

16. Barrymore was named after its owner, Lord Barrymore.

17. These modern houses occupy the site of Lord Barrymore's theatre.

18. The St George and Dragon pub, former hotel, boatyard and wharf.

19 & 20. The landing stages for two of the several ferries which enabled people, goods and animals to cross the river.

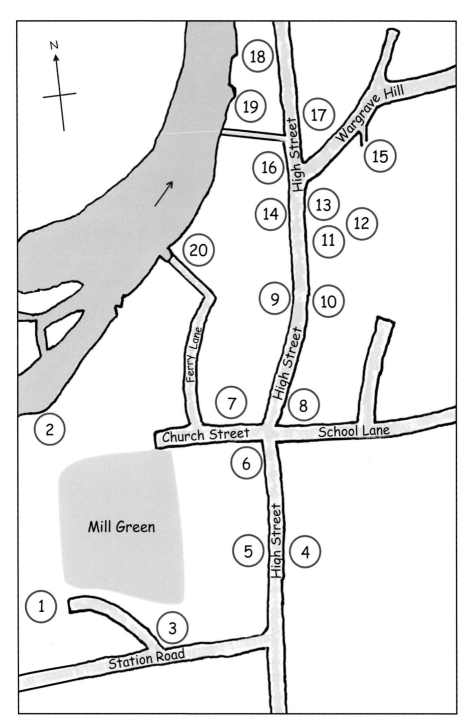

Shops and businesses

In common with the majority of villages, a major change during recent years has been the decline in the number of local shops and services, but a hundred years ago the High Street and Victoria Road were bustling with shops and businesses. Those were the days before widely accessible public and private transport, which meant that all one's normal household needs would have been met within the village. Walking down Victoria Road, past the shops and Frank Pope's plant nursery and then along the High Street, might have reminded us of the nursery rhyme reference to 'the butcher, the baker and the candlestick maker'.

Old newspapers and early photographs in our Local History Society archives highlight some of the wide range of businesses that have traded in or around the High Street or Victoria Road over the years including:

Antiques • Art Gallery • Bakers • Banks • Beauty Salon

Blacksmith • Butchers • Cane Furniture • Car Sales • Chemist

Coffee Shops • Confectioners • Corn Merchant • Cruise & Dine

Cycle Builder • Dairies • Dance Studio • Dentist • Draper

Electrical Goods • Estate Agents • Fishmonger • Fitness Studio

Florist • Garages • Greengrocers • Grocers • Hairdressers

Newsagents • Post Offices • Pubs/Inns • Radios • Restaurants

Seed Merchant • Shoe Repairs • Handbags • Stabling • Taxi Hire

Tea Rooms • Tobacconists • Toys & Games • Upholstery

Mr Richardson stands proudly outside his High Street shop with its impressive display of fresh meat. Although the development of commercial refrigeration in the later years of the nineteenth century made it feasible to import beef from South America, the technology had not yet reached retail businesses or private homes. Housewives had to buy perishable items, such as meat and fish, more frequently, especially during warmer weather. The 'fleet' of delivery vehicles stands ready to serve the village.

J. Richardson, Family Butcher & Poulterer, Wargrave.
Families waited upon daily for orders

Just across the road from Mr Richardson's shop, there was a branch of International Stores, a nationwide chain of grocers. Every town would have had one or more branches and you could even find them in villages such as ours. Other national chains were represented too. Although it's not easy to spot, you might have noticed in the photograph above that the shop next door to Mr Richardson is a branch of W H Smith, the

newsagent and stationer. Some time later, they outgrew this shop and moved to larger premises across the road.

Three national banks also had branches in the village, together with two post offices.

Next door to the International Stores, you can see Timber Cottage, mentioned earlier, with its sign inviting us to sample the delights on offer in the Tea Parlour.

15

The former White Hart Hotel was one of the seven public houses which were open along the High Street at one time. It is now a restaurant. The old petrol pump which is there today reminds us that the driveway used to lead up to Wargrave Service Garage, run by the Rideout family. Eventually, the business closed down and smart new houses took its place, as more recently happened to Wargrave Motors, further along the High Street.

Harry Barker's bakery was at the bottom of Church Street, near to the 'kissing gate' at the entrance to Mill Green. Not only was he selling his freshly-baked products, his shop window is also advertising other delights such as Cadbury's chocolate and Fry's cocoa.

This photograph was taken very early in the 1900s and the newly-opened Woodclyffe Hall, together with its splendid gas lamppost, is the latest arrival to join the wide range of architectural styles in the High Street.

Notice that there is no well-defined footpath, so the lady in the foreground is having to pick her way carefully, especially as almost all the wheeled traffic was horse-drawn.

The Barrymore story

Many interesting people have lived in Wargrave, but one of the most unusual and socially prominent in the eighteenth century was Lord Barrymore, whose house of the same name stands at the northern end of the High Street. He came from a wealthy Irish family and was a leading light in the Georgian social scene, with a passion for gambling and the theatre. He bought this fine house and, in 1788, built a large theatre across the road and invited his London friends, including the Prince of Wales. Although wealthy, he could not afford his lifestyle and

eventually faced bankruptcy. His creditors stripped the theatre and it was later demolished. Undaunted, he then joined the Berkshire Militia as a Captain, but was killed when his musket discharged accidentally. He was buried in an unmarked grave at St Mary's church in Wargrave. He was only 23 years old.

The theatre was reputed to seat an audience of several hundred people and was one of the largest in the country. To house some of the visitors, simple dormitory accommodation was built in the High Street just along from Barrymore. This was later converted to a long row of individual cottages which are still standing.

LORD BARYMORES THEATRE AT WARGRAVE

The Woodclyffe story

This is the story of a remarkable Victorian lady whose outstanding generosity continues to have an important influence on village life today.

Harriette Cooke Smith was born in 1824 and was the daughter of the Reverend James Hitchings who became the Vicar of Wargrave two years later. He died in 1850 and Harriette and her mother moved from the Vicarage to Orchard House on the High Street until, at the age of 33, she married her cousin William Smith, a wealthy London businessman. She was often known as Harriette Cooke Smith; by coincidence, both her mother's and mother-in-law's maiden names were Cooke.

For much of their married life the Smiths lived and worked in London but in 1869 they also bought a cottage at the edge of the village on the Henley Road, it was then called *Hill Side*. They greatly extended the house in typical Victorian Gothic style with strong influences of the Arts & Crafts Movement and renamed it *Woodclyffe*. The house became their summer retreat where Harriette involved herself in village activities. She was an accomplished artist and enjoyed painting scenes of riverside life.

William Smith died in October 1899 and was buried at St Mary's church in Wargrave. In the spring of the next year, it was announced that Mrs Smith was planning to build a village hall in her husband's memory.

For more than 100 years, the Woodclyffe Hall has provided an ideal venue for a remarkable range of events and activities. The portraits of William and Harriette hang in the main hall: silent witnesses to a vibrant and energetic community.

In the early years of the twentieth century, Harriette made a series of generous gifts which have proved to be of lasting value to the village, including the Woodclyffe Hostel. After serving as a convalescent ward during the First World War, the Hostel now houses the library, snooker club and Theatre Workshop.

The most attractive Woodclyffe Almshouses off Wargrave Hill were established in 1902 and the six-acre allotments off Victoria Road were opened in 1903. Harriette gave a further 11 acres in 1907 for the Recreation Ground, complete with a pavilion and a groundsman's house. The old pavilion is now the Parish Council office.

Harriette Cooke Smith made a major contribution to the strengthening of our village community through her thoughtful gifts which have brought tangible benefits to ordinary village folk for a very long time.

Wargrave at war

The 69 names inscribed on the War Memorial cross on Mill Green remind us of the sacrifice made by so many families in two World Wars. The names of the fallen are read out at the annual Remembrance Day service. Here we see the unveiling of the memorial in May 1921 by Field Marshal Sir William Robertson.

The First World War

As the grim reality of trench warfare in France took its toll, emergency convalescent hospitals were set up in many towns and villages to cope with the large number of wounded soldiers. The Woodclyffe Hostel was set up as a recovery hospital by the local Wargrave Red Cross Voluntary Aid Detachment. The plaque on the front of the building records their dedication. A story is told that some of the soldiers were decidedly uneasy when they were told the name of the village to which they were being sent! Later, the Woodclyffe Hall was taken over to be the main ward and the Hostel was used as common and dining rooms. The photograph was taken in the Hall and, as demand grew, a third row of beds was installed down the centre.

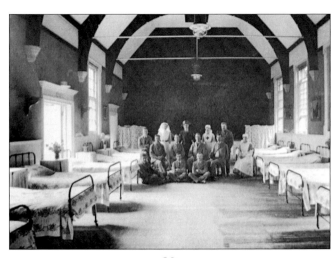

The Second World War

Thankfully, the village was not affected by any direct enemy action during the Second World War, but everyday life certainly changed. As well as local men being called up for military service, villagers had to cope with food rationing, the threat of air raids and preparations for a possible invasion. There were new faces at the schools: children evacuated from London to avoid the bombing. In common with villages throughout the country, a Home Guard platoon was formed, their training focused on preparations for the threatened German invasion.

A turning point in the war came later when the USA joined the fight and we began to think of an invasion of mainland Europe by Allied troops. From that time onwards, the military presence was felt everywhere. A field at the top of Victoria Road was prepared as a camp for American troops training for D-Day, the invasion of Normandy.

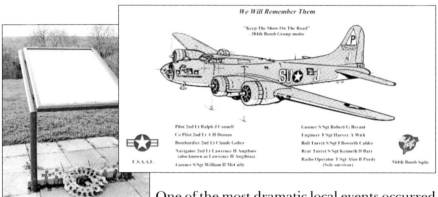

One of the most dramatic local events occurred in November 1943 when an American B17 'Flying Fortress' bomber broke up in mid-air and wreckage was scattered over the water meadows and in the river. Sadly, only one member of the 10-man crew was able to parachute to safety. A memorial stands near to Hennerton golf clubhouse.

Peace at last

Not surprisingly, there was widespread celebration when the war in Europe ended in May 1945. Wargrave children had a tea at the Woodclyffe Hall, followed by sports and a bonfire at the Recreation Ground. It was later decided that site of the American camp at the top of Victoria Road would be used for houses, giving us Highfield Park.

After six long years of war, a new version of village life was slowly emerging.

21

Outlying communities

The Parish of Wargrave includes a number of smaller communities, each with its own distinctive identity.

Crazies Hill
The unusual name of this small village is said to derive from an old word for buttercups. Its location on high ground meant that water supply was always a problem and Rebecca's Well used to be the hamlet's main source of drinking water. It was greatly improved by the local curate in 1870 who arranged the building of the handsome and useful structure, later decorated by the artist Gertrude Jekyll with an appropriate scene from the book of Genesis in the Bible.

The modern community has its own highly-regarded primary school and village hall but in earlier times it had to look to Wargrave for these amenities. The first school was opened in 1861 and remained in use for about 100 years. The village hall was originally a Mission Church. It also has an old, attractive and well supported pub, The Horns.

There are several interesting houses in the community, including Crazies Hall, which is set in extensive grounds and gardens. It was originally the Town Hall in Henley-on-Thames but was dismantled and moved to its present site by Major Willis in 1898 when the new and larger Town Hall was built. The Major's new house, called Crazies, incorporated the facade, cupola and formal entrance of the old building.

Hare Hatch, Kiln Green and Knowl Hill

These communities owe their existence to their positions along the Bath Road, which had for centuries provided one of the main routes from London to the West Country. When this was adopted as a Turnpike in the 18th century, communication by coach to the social life of Bath and the trading centre of Bristol was much improved, encouraging the gentry to build substantial and elegant houses along the road which we know as the A4. So Hare Hatch House, Hill House, Bear Place, Linden Hill, Scarletts and Castlemans sprang up.

One of the larger local houses which has survived is Yeldall Manor, near the junction of Blakes Road and Tag Lane on the eastern side of the village.

These new houses needed a large complement of staff, which led to the building of cottages, often 'tied' to the occupiers' employment.

The needs of travellers along this busy road encouraged the development of businesses, especially coaching inns, blacksmiths and trades associated with horse-drawn transport. Many of the travellers were prosperous or wealthy which created obvious economic opportunities. Businesses which have survived include the Bird in Hand, the New Inn, Knowl Hill Garage and the Horse and Groom at Hare Hatch, shown below.

This photograph includes a very early motor car, two horses and two bicycles. The building on the left is advertising 'Good stabling'.

Famous names

A number of well-known people have been associated with Wargrave over the years, here are some of them:

Dave Allen
Irish comedian and satirist with successful TV show from the late 1960s until the mid-1980s. Controversially irreverent towards authority.

Angela Baddeley
Stage and television actress, best remembered for her role as the household cook in the period TV drama *Upstairs, Downstairs*.

Lord Barrymore
Famous Georgian rake, hellraiser, gambler, sportsman and spendthrift. Built a large theatre in Wargrave. Led a short but eventful life.

Bert Bushnell
The Bushnell family has run a boatyard in the village for more than 100 years. Bert won a gold medal in the double sculls at the 1948 Olympics.

Paul Daniels
International magician, entertainer and TV star. A generous supporter and enthusiastic participant in village life. Partnered by Debbie McGee.

Peter Davison
TV actor appearing in several series, including Tristan in *All Creatures Great and Small* and as the Doctor in the BBC series *Doctor Who*.

Sandra Dickinson
American-British actress who has appeared in films as well as on TV. At the time she lived in Wargrave she was married to Peter Davison.

Emma
Queen of England in 1002, wife of King Ethelred and mother of Edward the Confessor. Is said to have had a home in Wargrave.

Bud Flanagan
Popular music hall entertainer. Appeared in shows for the troops at the Woodclyffe Hall during the war. Leader of The Crazy Gang.

Mary Hopkin
Welsh folk singer and actress with her own TV series. Represented UK in Eurovision Contest. Best known for her record *Those Were the Days*.

Gertrude Jekyll
A leading horticulturist, garden designer, writer and artist. Created more than 400 gardens here and abroad in the Victorian and Edwardian eras.

Sir Edwin Lutyens
International architect. Never lived in Wargrave but a close friend of the Hannen family. Designed the Cenotaph and also our War Memorial.

Debbie McGee
Famous TV, radio and stage performer. Best known as assistant to Paul Daniels. Outstanding dancer and regular broadcaster on local radio.

Sir Morrell McKenzie
Leading physician recommended by Queen Victoria to treat the Crown Prince of Prussia. He was knighted but, sadly, his patient didn't survive.

Kenneth More
Well known film, TV and stage actor. Became a star with *Genevieve*, followed by *The Forsyte Saga, Reach for the Sky* and many others.

Robert Morley
Stage and film actor. Starred in numerous films, usually playing a pompous English gentleman. A great supporter of village events.

Norman Rees
TV news reporter for 30 years with ITN, covering war zones around the globe including the Falklands. USA correspondent for four years.

Wargrave Local History Society

We hope that you have enjoyed reading this brief guide to the history of our village.

The Society was founded in 1981 with the aim of encouraging an interest in history, particularly in our local area and community. We have an extensive archive of documents and artefacts and have published five books.

We meet on the second Tuesday evening of each month, except in July and August, and hear a variety of guest speakers. Details of our programme are published in the Wargrave News.

Visitors are most welcome and you are invited to become a full member. To find out more about the Society, visit our website:

www.wargravehistory.org.uk

Our meetings are held in the Old Pavilion at the Recreation Ground, both of which were gifts from Harriette Cooke Smith.